First published in Great Britain in 2006
by Weidenfeld & Nicolson
10 9 8 7 6 5 4 3 2 1

Text copyright © Kaiser Chiefs
Design and layout copyright © Weidenfeld & Nicolson 2006

A CIP catalogue record for this book is available from
the British Library.

ISBN-13: 978-1-841-88268-1
ISBN-10: 1-841-88268-2

Designed and art directed by Cally
Text reported to Imran Ahmed

Printed and bound in the UK

Weidenfeld & Nicolson
The Orion Publishing Group Ltd
Orion House
5 Upper St Martin's Lane
London WC2H 9EA

The Orion Publishing Group's policy is to use papers that
are natural, renewable and recyclable products and made
from wood grown in sustainable forests. The logging and
manufacturing processes are expected to conform to the
environmental regulations of the country of origin.

A RECORD OF EMPLOYMENT

WEIDENFELD & NICOLSON

"... a lot of that time was spent doing these terrible London gigs. It was made worse because we had these stupid day jobs." RICKY

Ricky: When we first started, people were saying things like, "Well, we don't really get it," because it didn't sound like anything and we'd go, "Well, that's a start". Even if it's shit, at least it's not like anything! I remember we did our second ever gig supporting Franz Ferdinand at The Cockpit. It felt like a bit of a backlash against the American rock revolution that was around at the time.

Simon: I remember we wrote a couple of songs, I think 'Oh My God' was the first we wrote, and it was like, yes! I think we knew to some extent then that we'd kind of got what we wanted sound-wise.

Ricky: It was quite exciting but at the same time a lot of that time was spent doing these terrible London gigs. It was made worse because we had these stupid day jobs. We had to get off work at midday, go down to London, come back the same night and work the next day. What was funny was every time we went down, no record industry turned up! But we were always getting people on board. It was exciting because we were getting a team together and getting some fans together.

Simon: So even when we were playing in London, we could be guaranteed that we weren't going to just turn up and play to nobody. And in Leeds we could play to a decent sized number of people.

Ricky: We avoided a lot of the stuff that was popular at the time and we were never one of the cool bands. I don't know how we came across as cool! I think we were far too cool for the cool set!

RADAR

SEEKING OUT THE BEST IN NEW MUSIC
Edited by Imran Ahmed

NEWS

REACH FOR THE CZARS!

Radar travels to Russia to spend 48 hours in the whirlwind of weirdness that is Leeds' Kaiser Chiefs

Here at *NME*, things don't always go as planned. Take this Kaiser Chiefs interview, for example. Our aim was simple enough: to ask them how it felt when – after we put the demo of their debut single 'Oh My God' on the *NME* stereo last year – 20 record companies started kissing their arses and throwing chequebooks at them. We wanted to ask about Pigs, the club night that Ricky Wilson (vocals), Andrew White (guitar), Simon Rix (bass), Nick 'Peanut' Baines (keyboard) and Nick Hodgson (drums) run in Leeds that's so debauched the bouncers have banned them from playing Motörhead's 'Ace Of Spades' for fear of riots. And we wanted to mention how their wobbly art-pop skilfully pogos its way across the back catalogues of The Clash, Madness, Blur and the Super Furry Animals. But we can't. Because what happened when we caught up with them in Russia was so bizarre we didn't need to interview them at all...

Friday, July 30, 10.04pm
Moscow Airport

The band and *NME* are greeted at the airport, not by a rickety old tour van but a bona fide governmental car, sent to pick us up on order of the fucking *Kremlin!* Clearly the Russians take this band's arrival very seriously.

Saturday, July 31, 7.53pm
Fender Fest

The Kaiser Chiefs play a storming set for thousands of bouncing Muscovites. Russian festivals aren't much like the ones we have in Britain. Instead of hash cakes, silly hats and poorly-pitched tents, you get hardnuts from the Russian army kicking the crap out of anyone who dares to mosh. During sets by King Adora and Gold Blade, unarmed skinny indie kids are dragged out and pummelled by uniformed oafs. But strangely, the army grunts declare an official ceasefire and actually start *dancing* during the Kaisers' set.

"They seem to be one of our biggest fanbases," says Ricky, gobsmacked as he spots a young soldier whistling the chorus to 'Oh My God' while polishing his Kalashnikov. "I guess they're mesmerised by my stage presence."

Why has everyone here gone gonzo over you lot?

Nick: "Well, you could say it's because we have catchy choruses that go, *'Oh oh oh!'*"

Ricky: "Or because Russians know how to spot ultimate party music."

Nick: "But, really, I think it's just because we're fit."

Saturday, July 31, 9.12pm
Fender Fest Aftershow

Perhaps that explains why, backstage, the band are getting stalked by Russia's answer to Madonna. As the paparazzi frantically try to snap her, she kidnaps Ricky, takes him off to a spot by the riverside and whispers seductively in his ear, "All I want to do is suck dick."

Ricky's a little nervous. "It's very flattering for your first stalker to be a billionaire Russian pop star," he says, after making his escape. "But she was making these weird bubbling noises and reckoned she'd been reincarnated as a king."

Saturday, July 31, 10.02pm
Fender Fest Aftershow

Suddenly the band are swamped by journos, liggers and TV cameras, all of whom want to give them Russian dolls as gifts. Bemused, the boys do their first proper TV interview ever to an estimated audience of just how amazing the Kaiser Chiefs are.

Sunday, August 1, 2.24am
Chinese Pilots

A vodka-soaked night is spent dancing in an underground drinking den with hundreds of Russian models fawning over the band. We grab a word to see why they're infatuated with the Kaisers.

"We met Craig Nicholls in France," says Olga, who's 21 and looks like a sexy cartoon squirrel. "He wouldn't stop talking about them."

Independently, a further three girls claim that Craig Nicholls turned them on to the Kaisers in France. It's not clear if The Vines have even *played* in France lately, suggesting that Craig goes on self-funded propaganda tours to spread the word about just how amazing the Kaiser Chiefs are.

Confused? Well, it's only just begun. If one DIY single, recorded in their shabby bedrooms, can generate this much madness, who knows what'll happen now that they've just signed to B-Unique?

"We'll be handed the keys to the Kremlin by 2005," declares Nick, triumphantly.

Is that possible?

"Definitely," beams Ricky with a confident smile. "After all, 100,003,072 Russians and Craig Nicholls can't be wrong." **Tim Jonze**

ANDY TAYLOR

> ### "We'll be handed the keys to the Kremlin by 2005"
> Ricky Wilson

Eastern Bloc party: Kaiser Chiefs (l-r) Nick Baines, Simon, Ricky, Nick Hodgson and Andrew rock Russia

---

Moscow, June 2004

Simon: We got asked to go play at a Russian festival because this guy called Sacha read about us in *Time Out*. He could've ended up with anyone. We thought it was one of those things where we pay for ourselves to go and don't get paid, but he paid for us and the hotel and all that. We just couldn't really tell what the catch was.

"They might as well have been The Beatles" TIM JONZE (NME)

Ricky: It was totally surreal. The first time we'd played outside England you know. The first time we'd played outside Leicester!

Tim Jonze (NME journo): They were really excited to be there and laughing at how surreal it all seemed. They weren't even signed at the time and nobody knew them in Britain, yet all these Russians were treating them like rock royalty. We all felt like we were blagging it, basically. But then they played and it went down amazingly. People were singing all the words to songs they can't have heard before. People were crowd surfing too, even though crowd surfing meant you were guaranteed to get dragged off by the Russian army (who were acting as security guards). They had a trail of girls following them around after that, and ended up doing these massive television interviews. They might as well have been The Beatles.

You could tell from Russia they were going to get big — their songs had that anthemic quality to them and people felt like they knew them from the minute they started. I guess Russians are just a bit quicker to catch on than people in the UK.

Note the Kaizer Chiefs
football team sticker

Peanut wore this shirt a lot
at early gigs. Pre-suits.

"because of the
badge Nick thinks
my jacket has
a John Smeaton
connection... but
there isn't.
I bought it for
two pounds in
Dundee" RICKY

"I have
suspiciously
wet crotch
here" RICKY

"We always wanted to take someone on tour that we were into" PRESTON

Preston (Ordinary Boys): I first heard the Kaiser Chiefs when someone sent me a demo. We always wanted to take someone on tour that we were into. We had a huge stack of demos for tour supports and I remember reading this tiny, tiny Kaiser Chiefs review in the NME that mentioned The Specials and Madness or whatever. So I stuck the CD on and really liked it.

I can remember some gigs that we did together in really weird places and tiny venues. No one would really show up and these gigs would be such non-events. Yet every night they would have so much energy.

'I Predict A Riot' always blew me away. We thought it was well Ramonesy. We'd be playing a venue with 13 people standing at the back talking really loudly and me, (Ordinary Boys guitarist) Will and (ex-drummer) Chuck moshing like fucking idiots at the front. Then they would return the favour for us.

I think people worry too much about what's cool and in vogue and the music bypasses that a little bit too much and I think that's what Kaiser Chiefs prove. Although I was more enthusiastic about them than most people, it never occurred to me that it would become the phenomenon it did. They haven't changed at all. I think because they knew it was going to happen all along, they're unaffected by the success.

"Preston has much better clothes since he was on Big Brother." RICKY

> **"I was sick onstage at Leeds, then they made us clean it up"**
>
> RICKY

Reading / Leeds Festival, August 2004

Peanut: The tent was more packed in Leeds than in Reading. The south hadn't really caught on yet. The mouths in London hadn't said yes, go watch this band, but in Leeds they were just happy we were from there and plenty of the festival goers were keen to see us.

Simon: We were very pleased to get on the Reading / Leeds festival. We weren't on first but very early. I thought it was alright, though there were a lot of Kaiser Chiefs football team flags in the crowd.

Simon: We did get better as the year went on, playing to more fans and also from doing more gigs. I remember both in Reading and Leeds there was a good number of people. I don't think we sounded amazing or anything like that, but I thought we were good. And the crowd obviously enjoyed it.

Ricky: That was back in my puking days. I used to be sick before I went on and after I came off. I was sick onstage at Leeds, then they made us clean it up with water bottles. Something went wrong with Whitey's guitar and he stopped playing. We weren't very good. But we probably thought we were.

"Instead of signing all these fucking crap bands that you're signing, you should sign the Kaiser Chiefs, they're brilliant!"

PRESTON – THE ORDINARY BOYS

Mark Lewis (B-Unique – independent record label): I went to see The Ordinary Boys in Bristol and got an absolute mouthful from Preston: "Instead of signing all these fucking crap bands that you're signing, you should sign the Kaiser Chiefs, they're brilliant!"

It struck a real chord with me. And I saw them and I thought yeah, they're fucking great, they were just brilliant. It wasn't the best gig but you could just tell they had that thing about them.

Paul Harris (B-Unique): There was a night in Leeds that was the first time all three of us had seen them together. We have a thing at B-Unique that the three of us all have to agree on something before we sign them. So we went to see them at The Cockpit, which was just mental, it was the most rammed gig and they were headlining it. There was no turning back at that point, it was just like – we've got to fucking do this.

Martin Toher (B-Unique): That gig was really mad because there were about 450 people there! To see an unsigned band playing to that many people it was just ridiculous... you could feel something was going on.

Mark: If you're talking about indie deals, it was by far the biggest we'd ever done. For us it was a lot of money. It was definitely make or break for the label. Our plan actually really revolved around getting the Kaisers a second Ordinary Boys tour. We planned to get on The Ordinary Boys tour, get 'Riot' in the Top 40, and then just roll on from there, it was really basic stuff.

Martin: We were spending a lot of money, major record company level money in making the record and the videos. We'd set ourselves a realistic target and hoped to sell somewhere between 60,000 and 100,000 albums. That was the target. We thought if they could sell 100,000 albums then that would be incredible! We've sold nearly 2 million now!

"I bought this tie in Tie Rack at Heathrow. I don't like it much" NICK

"I never enjoyed playing the Barfly. The day usually included driving to London and back with no luck. At least they gave us free Evian" RICKY

Time Honoured Tradition

I Predict a Riot

Modern Way

Oh My God

Saturday Night

Na Na Na Na Na Naaa

Everyday I love u less and less

Born To Be A Dancer

You Can Have It All

Hard Times Send Me

Stephen Street 'Employment' co-producer

"I thought, there is something special here, there is that energy I saw when I first saw Blur"

"I think my favourite Kaiser Chiefs song would have to be 'I Predict A Riot' cos it's the first one we ever did together.

"I first met the Kaisers when I went to see an Ordinary Boys gig and the Kaiser Chiefs were supporting them. After the gig this kinda tallish chap with a nice smart haircut came up to me and said, 'Are you Stephen?' and it was Nick from the Kaiser Chiefs. He gave me a CD to listen to.

"I think they wanted to work with me because they were big fans of all the Blur stuff. I think they felt my sensibilities matched theirs, as far as they wanted to be alternative but at the same time they wanted to have some decent pop production. When I say pop I don't mean pop as in Atomic Kitten – something to make it sound melodic and rhythmically strong, y'know?

"The best bands I've worked with, be it Blur or The Smiths, the bands have a natural chemistry between each other. That's why they work as a band. It doesn't have to be completely democratic but there has to be a natural balance. Like if you had a band full of Nicks for instance, it wouldn't work would it? If you had a band full of Morrisseys it wouldn't work. You've got to have people who have a natural balance. I thought they had that straight away. I thought there is something special here, there is that energy I saw when I first saw Blur."

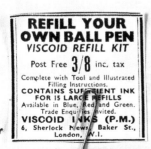

"Stick to the bass, Curley..." PEANUT

"I think we used to make too much of an effort fashion wise. There was even a coathanger on stage. Peanut's scarf was the first thing to go"

RICKY

"Damon Albarn stole all my moves..." RICKY

Steve Harris 'Employment' co-producer

"I got the tape rolling, and it was like that's genius, absolutely genius"

"The Kaiser track that I think is a really great song is 'Modern Way'. I think 'Riot' is up there with anything The Jam have done, as a pop song it'll stay around forever.

"I first met the Kaiser Chiefs through a really good friend of mine, my manager (and one of the Kaiser Chiefs' label bosses) Martin Toher. At first I was only asked to do B-sides in Leeds.

"I had no idea who these people were. I was in the studio at 10 o'clock, shook hands, 'Hi, I'm going to be producing your B-sides.' Off we go. And I think Martin really did it as a get-to-know-you session more than anything. I got the tape rolling, and it was like: that's genius, absolutely genius. Their energy and vibe blew me away.

"Nick was the driving force of those B-side sessions and he was very good at quick decision making. That's what producers like me really need, somebody who knows what they want and inspires us to go and get it.

"When I went to see them live that sealed it for me, at this little club at the back of Rock City, Nottingham. There were 125, 150 people there max and I've never seen anything like it. There was sheer excitement in the crowd, they were just going mental. I really felt like jumping around! I was thinking, this is a fucking great song. And I was jumping up and down by that point, and I think that's when Martin said, 'Do you wanna do that song, and some more songs on the album?'"

"There was sheer excitement in the crowd, they were just going mental"

Steve Harris

'I don't have a clue where or when this was taken. But it must have been the same day we all bought razors.' RICKY

"Here we are, in the fucking charts!"

NICK

Nick: One of the things we found when we were putting this scrap book together was a list of 16 songs. And at the bottom in different pen, number 17, was 'I Predict A Riot'. The 17th song we wrote! I was surprised at that.

Peanut: Everything up to 'I Predict A Riot' was us finding our way. That then became our way.

Nick: I think what would've happened without it is we would have had a medium indie career, sold a medium amount of records and played medium sized venues.

Simon: It doesn't sound like any other band. Some of our songs could be written by other bands but 'I Predict A Riot' and 'Oh My God', those two in particular are individual to us in their sound.

Stephen Street (producer): At the end of our first ever session together we had this fantastic version of 'I Predict a Riot' which I knew we'd done a good job on but never imagined in my wildest dreams it would go on to be as successful as it was. The version that is still played to this day is the very first we did in the studio, in the bunker. We just managed to hit some magic that week.

I remember us listening back to 'I Predict A Riot' and Ricky stood in the corner of the room and said, "I'd never heard myself sound like that before!" Well, that's what you sound like mate, it's great!

Steve Harris (producer): I remember the first time 'Riot' went in the Top 40. We were recording other tracks on 'Employment' and had a radio on in the studio. And the five of them just got into a huddle and put their heads down and had a very private moment. I found it really touching. Maybe 'cos they weren't young kids and had worked hard, had done it for years. And I couldn't wish it to five nicer people.

Nick: I've never told anyone this before, but what I said in the huddle was, "We've been doing this for years and here we are, in the fucking charts!" And everyone started crying. Well, me, Ricky and Whitey definitely cried.

"The NME tour was an important
turning point for us because we
gathered a lot of new fans."
PEANUT

"The stripey blazers are long gone!" NICK

"I seem to have two looks.
Blue suit with jacket on and blue
suit with jacket off. Here I am
sporting the latter" RICKY

Recording 'Employment', December 2004

Ricky: We recorded the album in two halves. Half at a studio in Lincolnshire called The Chapel with Steve Harris. And the other half with Stephen Street in London.

Stephen Street: B-Unique said they wanted me to do the whole album but I couldn't. I'd have loved to but I was working on a New Order album at the time. Much as I'd have loved to do the whole album I just had two weeks, so I asked if we could concentrate on doing the mixes of the tracks I'd done so far and two or three other tracks. I said I had always liked 'Saturday Night' as well and 'Modern Way' so I did nick the good ones but then again I was first there!

"I felt that the demos were a bit psychedelic, dare I say it, a bit Syd Barrett-y" STEPHEN STREET

I felt that the demos were a bit psychedelic, dare I say it, a bit Syd Barrett-y, in that everything was very tracked vocally. I felt it was good but a bit hazy. I wanted to try and bring Ricky's social exuberance more to the fore.

There was a little bit of finishing off needed on the songs, otherwise there'd be no point me being there. Obviously, I tried a few different things. On 'Everyday I Love You Less And Less' I got Nick to do the staggered drumming bit at the beginning rather than playing all the way through the beginning, and dropping out for the first line of the second verse so it drops down a bit, (sings) "Everyday I love you less and less" and the kick comes in again - things like that, little tricks that give it a bit more dynamics.

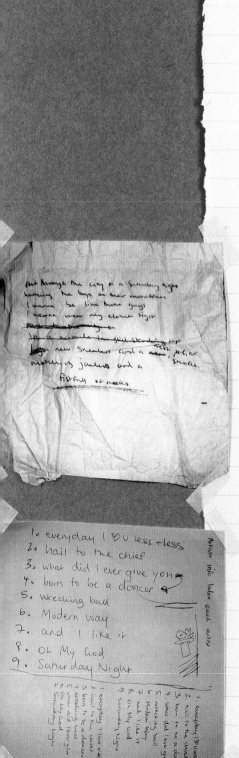

"Nick is the drummer and the main songwriter which you don't often get with bands" STEPHEN STREET

They were very open and responsive in the studio. Obviously it's a bit of a strange set-up because Nick is the drummer and the main songwriter which you don't often get with bands. Nick would be very concerned that it was the right tempo because he was used to playing them faster live. Once we'd settled on the actual tempo of the track Nick was very open to trying out new suggestions and things.

One of the things I wanted to bring out a little bit more which wasn't so prevalent on the demos was Whitey's guitar work because he's a very strong guitarist. The keyboards that Peanut plays are just as important. Peanut is the boffin in the band. Up to that point he'd been in charge of doing lots of engineering on the demos, coming up with the little sounds and things. In fact, a lot of the weird sounds, guitar-y and other effects he'd manage to put in the demos we actually lifted them for 'Employment'. It saved us from having to set up and do them all over again and they sounded great. I found it quite refreshing, we weren't looking to obliterate everything with guitars, we were leaving a bit of space there for some of Peanut's keyboards and Simon's a very solid bass player, really good, very groovy.

Obviously the other main thing is working on the vocals and making sure they sound great. And as I was saying, the more I got to know Ricky the more I saw a really great frontman there. He just grew in confidence. They ticked all the boxes.

Simon: The Chapel is really remote. There's a pub, one. It's in Lincolnshire. There's about three or four houses and a graveyard.

Ricky: We had quite a good time at the graveyard. We started daring people to walk through it late at night. I was half way around and Euan who was an engineer at Chapel jumped out from behind a grave stone – "Whoooooaaa!" I've never been so scared I've fallen over before! Mark (Lewis) and Martin (Toher) from our label came up to visit one time and did the graveyard run. Mark took a snooker cue round and Martin had a sock with a snooker ball in it. As if they're gonna fight ghosts with a snooker cue!

Peanut: There were a few days where it was really strange. We did feel quite isolated. But you didn't ever have to worry about anything. You sleep, you eat, you record and that's it. If we had wanted to we could have recorded 24 hours a day.

Whitey: I really loved recording in Chapel. It's the image I've always had of bands recording, in the country, isolated from everywhere and just the band and the producer and that's it.

Simon: The thing we liked about the Chapel was we recorded there for two and a half, three weeks and we recorded solidly, bang, bang, bang, did it. But then when we were doing it with Stephen Street we kept doing a song and then going on tour for two weeks. The whole recording of 'Employment' was quite broken up because we kept touring.

"Whitey went out for cigarettes and came back with a motorbike" STEVE HARRIS

Steve Harris: I had them for three weeks. And I think it was the first time for a long time where they actually just settled down and relaxed and didn't have to do anything, 'cos there's nothing to do except record or go down the pub. The atmosphere was great. I think they really enjoyed that time. My favourite moment of those sessions and probably favourite Kaiser Chiefs moment of the last 12 months was during the recording of the album. Whitey went out for a packet of cigarettes and came back with a motorbike. It was one of those mini-motos and he broke it within a day.

Whitey: Yeah I did, yeah. It was a bit of a mistake to be honest. It was on the seafront and they've got these naff kind of tat shops. You know the little mini motorbike things? The quite cheap ones that you have to sit right down on? I brought it back and everybody was disgusted. Because it's just another thing that I buy, I tend to buy ridiculous things or stuff I don't necessarily need. Like 20 guitars, 20 scooters, that kind of thing. But it stopped working after two days, I took it back and got a refund.

"'Employment' would be a great name for an album" NICK

Simon: Everyone else seemed to enjoy recording at Chapel, to be having a really good time. I thought it was like being on a really bad geography field trip.

Stephen Street: I think one of the only sticking points was 'Everyday I Love You Less And Less'. Nick wasn't convinced the version I'd done was fast enough. So they cut a new version with Steve (Harris) and played it back to me in the studio.

Steve Harris: We had another crack at 'Everyday I Love You Less and Less', which is a corking version but it's more punk. And there was all this discussion about which version they should use. Steve's was very pop, and I think Steve went back and, sort of, toughened his up a little bit, and I know he sped it up a little. It works fantastic, and I'm really glad they went with that version because I think it's superior. But there's a cracking punk version of it as well somewhere.

Mark Lewis (B-Unique): We were quite conscious in the beginning that we didn't want the album to sound as if two different people had made it. Although I think if you listen to it, there is a difference in that Harris has done more expansive tracks, there's a sort of slight Beach Boys element to some of the stuff, isn't there? Stephen's tracks are more straight ahead and direct.

Ricky: Yeah I think having two producers worked. When I listen to the album it works quite well because having two people involved gave it more light and shade, you know?

Nick: It is true that my girlfriend, Anna came up with the album title. We were driving to my Mum and Dad's house listening to Blur's 'Leisure'. She said 'Me and my brother, used to describe 'Leisure' as an unemployment album'. And I said, unemployment. 'Employment' would be a great name for an album.

Simon: 'Employment' seemed to sum everything up for us at that time. We'd struggled to hold down jobs and be the Kaiser Chiefs but it all worked out. By contrast, the next album is looking like it's going to be called 'The Pub At Two'!

Tim Blackwell, Kaisers' filmmaker and friend

"I think my first impression of him was pretty much like, you know, he's a bit of a wanker."

"I met Ricky in the first week of college. I think I asked him which way it was to some kind of meeting and he made some quip and I think my first impression of him was pretty much like, you know, he's a bit of a wanker. But he grew on me, you realised it was just his way, it was just this confident performance. And he struck me as a very interesting character.

"Ricky would say, 'Oh, I'm in this band', so we piled down and watched them. I was quite taken back by how confident they were for a bunch of 18-year-olds. It's all relative to where they are now but I think they've always been confident in their own abilities. There was something quite immediately likeable about them.

"I've been filming them ever since their early days. I've got their first gigs as Parva on tape and I made their two promos as well back then. With the Kaisers I was there for a lot of the beginning and the build up. I filmed them at Leeds Festival 2004.

"He's the Neville Southall of the band."

"The guys have been in various bands together since they were in school, so rehearsals are very close knit, a lot of humour. It's quite well documented that Ricky and Nick are funny, but actually all the band are very funny in different ways. So rehearsals is this grappling of personalities, just a good bunch of people to hang out with. But they're quite professional about it too, when I say humour, they're not mucking around. It's just there's a lot of rubbish and silliness.

"It's kind of inevitable you get Ricky and Nick playing up to the camera the most. I think there's a friendly rivalry. They're both always trying to trump each other's jokes but at the same time feeding off each other as well. They're really great friends but it almost manifests itself as a friendly rivalry.

"Whitey's possibly the most reluctant of the five, but if anything he's the one most likely to snatch the camera from you and mess around with it. I think he's very much in it for the music and I think the other stuff, he knows that you have to go along with it now and it's part of the whole picture. He's the Neville Southall of the band."

'I Predict a Riot' Video, September 2004

"He was coughing up feathers after every take" CHARLIE PAUL

Charlie Paul, video director: The idea for the 'I Predict A Riot' video was developed from the band's request not to create a video full of confrontation, and to steer away from the negative aspect of a riot. So I tried not to interpret it literally but just get into a vibe with the music and pace of the track. Anyway, once you start to work with the lyrics you can't help but end up on the street in Leeds on a Saturday night! So I worked on the idea of how close can you get to a riot without any violence, and make it visually engaging.

'This was how the pillow idea evolved. This idea of a pillow fight party is now a reality and I have met a few people who have received a text as to where to meet and fight, often public spaces. The idea of a wind tunnel went with feathers perfectly, and that is it, all they had to do then was steal the pillows (which the band did in Camden Lock) and perform as they do live.

'All I did was give them the space to work in. They were completely open and enthusiastic about the whole thing. It was boiling hot, and we were packed to the ceiling with extras, the band worked like troupers and did take after take without a single complaint.

'Ricky's on-stage antics were inspired, and filled most of the screen time, even though he was coughing up feathers after every take! The whole band's performance was electrifying. The scene at the end of the shoot was amazing, feathers knee high and everywhere.

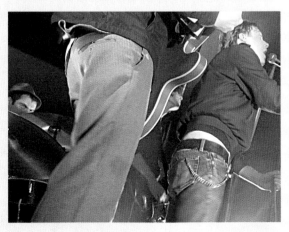

'I Predict A Riot' 16mm film 3.45 min

We open with the band, on stage, in a wind tunnel, they are backlit by massive bright white lamps, which are situated behind an enormous fan.

The guitar intro brings on a series of quick cut shots of what seem to be sofas, beds, waiting rooms, and Ikea salesrooms. All the shots are void of people, but have one thing in common, soft pillows and cushions. On the last shot of this section, a hand comes in and removes a cushion from a showroom display. Cut back to the band, the fan slowly turns behind them, casting dramatic shadows over their performance, there is a tongue-in-cheek look about this. Why are they playing to nobody on a set straight out of a Ridley Scott movie?

We cut back to our exterior shots, people are removing pillows and cushions from all over the place, hospital beds, bedrooms, Granny's wheelchair, all funny observational shots with characters (also using the band members as central characters). Even though these are all separate events they feel connected.

The travelling cushion carriers seem all to be heading in one direction, by bus, car, motorbike, scooter, skateboard, public transport and foot. We are amused by the comical situations these pillows create, on the tube with a big flowery cushion stuffed up your jumper, or jogging through a park with granny's lacy pillow under one arm, two people in a train station sharing a pillow to snooze on.

We cut back to the band who deliver a great performance in their stylish set with a cheeky nod to the '80s, but the relationship between the performance and the story line seem completely at odds with each other. That is until, on the second verse, they all start to pour into the room where the band is performing, carrying their precious pillows.

When the second verse kicks in, it all starts to kick off, and a massive pillow fight begins, feathers and down start to fly as the fight takes hold of the crowd, flashing lights and high speed film slows the action down, and freezes the tiny feathers and contorted faces.

Everyone is having a right laugh, and just as it couldn't get any crazier, the guitar solo comes in, this starts up the massive fan behind the band, which churns the atmosphere into a hurricane of feathers.

The band struggle to stay on their feet as the force ten gale sends the audience into a bigger frenzy, and as a viewer we can't help but wish we were there.

We stay with this scene throughout the rest of the song, using the settling of the feathers as a way to slow down, and by the end we have a stunned but exhilarated audience watching the band.

We cut the final band shots with some exterior scenes, our gig goers are heading home, everyone looks like they have been tarred and feathered, and as the track plays out, we leave with the comical sight of what looks like a load of fluff monsters, travelling in the wee hours, back in the direction from which they came.

"We didn't do this a lot.
Just me, Peanut and a $1/3$ of
a pint of piss" RICKY

NME Tour, January 2005

Martin Toher (B-Unique): It happened one Friday morning. I walked in the office and Mark said, "You won't believe this, but it looks like we're going to get on the NME tour!" I mean it never figured in our plans at all. That was a pure bonus.

Conor McNicholas (NME Editor): I first saw the Kaisers play the opening night of Club NME at Koko in Camden, September 2004. I was looking for an opening act for the NME Awards Tour. From the minute they took to the stage it was a done deal. They hit with such confidence and impact you were just blown away. They were perfect as an opener. I wanted a band that would rip people's heads off at 7:30 in the evening and get them away from the bar at a Student Union.

"The best tour I've ever known. Kaiser Chiefs, Bloc Party, The Futureheads, The Killers - imagine that!" NICK

Conor McNicholas: The rest of the tour was so strong - The Killers, Bloc Party, The Futureheads - that in a way, it didn't matter who opened. What became clear in the following weeks was that the Kaisers were cut from very different cloth from everyone else around. They had kicking tunes, an incredible work ethic, total commitment, the wisdom to see a plan and stick to it and an amazing set of characters in the band. It became clear that this was all set to go. By the time they hit the tour the magic opening slot had struck again and the whole bill started to feel upside down. They killed it every night, an amazing experience to see them.

Nick: The first slot was a great place to be, because we got to have more fun. For me personally that's the best tour I've ever known. Kaiser Chiefs, Bloc Party, The Futureheads, The Killers - imagine that! We definitely didn't feel like we were supporting - it's just like four bands of varying levels of success at the time. Weirdly, we were the oldest band on the bill.

"This is Brandon Flowers. He's the keyboard player in The Killers. He says something interesting on the next page" RICKY

Brandon Flowers (The Killers frontman): Over in the States they don't know about this NME tour that we did. I explained it was The Future-heads, Bloc Party, Kaiser Chiefs and The Killers for three weeks. They were amazed. Looking back, I think that tour was a great moment.

Ricky was the sparkle of those three weeks for me. He just has that gift of making you feel happy. We were headlining and in the middle of our set all of a sudden you'd see somebody crowd surfing and it would be Ricky. I remember meeting Ricky, Peanut and everybody and talking about how they enjoyed us and one of the reasons being they're not afraid to write pop songs. They do that very well, they're a rock band that plays pop music and they're not afraid of it and it comes across.

"I got blamed for his tie being put in some soup. I was a little be frightened"

BRANDON FLOWERS

Brandon Flowers: Once I was sitting next to Whitey and we were eating and somehow I got blamed for his tie being put in some soup. I was a little bit frightened cos he's a big man!

Whitey: To be honest, I can't remember everything about the tie in soup thing. I was in catering and everyone sits in their own spots and the table was full but there was an empty table next to it, so I sat on my own. And Brandon came in and sat next to me. We were a tiny band at the time. I was talking to him, very nice, very pleasant and I just realised that I'd had my tie in my soup for the entire conversation. For about five minutes he'd just been looking at me weirdly but he was too sweet to say anything.

What did I do after the NME tour? I went home and sanded floors. I rarely want to stay after gigs. The band is a massive part of my life, but not the only thing in my life. I've got a house and a girlfriend and a family and stuff. Plus, yeah, I'm quite old. I've done all my nightclubbing, I've done all my drug taking. I've seen every band I've wanted to see, more or less. So I just go home. Have a shit.

"This is just a picture of a tambourine. I think Peanut likes this photograph. He takes a lot of still lifes so appreciates it more than the rest of us" Ricky

'Oh My God', December 2004

"You can dance along, clap along or sing-a-long to it. It's all of those things." PEANUT

Nick: It's such a weird song. No one's done a song like that that's gone in the charts for years and years. Nobody does those nursery rhyme verses anymore - (sings) "Dehdeh-der-dur-dehdehdehdehdeh-der-deur".

Peanut: It's Pink Floyd-esque in the way that it bounced around - not that it's sad, you can dance along, clap along or sing-a-long to it. It's all of those things.

Whitey: If you listen to it, it is a weird song. It's got, what, a 20-second build up of screaming in the middle of it? When I say weird I mean it doesn't conform with classic songwriting.

Whitey: It's got a natural course. They flow when they're all finished and we're all playing our parts. But it's quite an awkward journey.

Simon: The chorus is still very catchy. And that's what allowed the verses to have all the licks and stuff. The chorus being very bang-bang-bang with a big thing to sing made it fine to do whatever we wanted for the rest of it.

"My favourite memories from the shoot include the band being chased by a yeti, Benny Hill style" CHARLIE PAUL

Nick: The B-Unique version of 'Oh My God' is my favourite video. I just think that took us longer, more early mornings and late nights than any of the others. The director was much more fastidious about every little measurement.

Charlie Paul (director): I like videos to treat songs literally, so the lyrics for 'Oh My God' led the way. The references to dead end jobs and wearing shirts with your "name tag" on them pointed to wanting to get away from it all, and inspired the store room scene, whereas the location scenes were built around the chorus.

The idea of the video was about how the band would find themselves in the furthest reaches of the planet, but that wasn't prophetic as it was obvious from my perspective they were going to be massive.

Some of my favourite memories from the shoot include the band being chased by a yeti, Benny Hill style, then having a massive bundle in the tent.

At the end of the shoot day in the toy storage depot, they did an acoustic version of 'Oh My God', and it was brilliant. Everyone had a massive smile on their faces and all the crew were spellbound – the gaffers even stopped talking to the riggers.

"Ricky's a cross between Iggy Pop and Norman Wisdom"

Tim Pope: Video Director and Argonaut.

"My favourite Kaisers song has to be 'I Predict A Riot'. You get this picture painted of what it's like up North, everyone falling out of fish 'n' chip shops and throwing up at chucking out time. And yet, there's a romantic kind of quality to it at the same time which I think is really interesting. It reminds me, and this may sound a little pretentious in print, but there's something about it that reminds me of how The Beatles observed stuff, like Northern stuff especially the Paul McCartney songs like 'Eleanor Rigby'.

"Some people think I
come across a bit smug"
RICKY

"The Kaisers originally asked me to do the storyboard for 'Oh My God'. But the idea I came up with was something way too wild at that point. It involved not much of the band, more of a dog running around or something

"But I ended up doing 'Everyday I Love You Less And Less'. There's this thing I love about the Kaisers' music which I think is very exhilarating. The raw, youthful energy of it. The bits where they scream – I think they're brilliant.

"On the day of the video shoot I remember Ricky being incredibly nervous. He kept going off to the loo and I thought – having worked with a lot of musicians – I know what he's up to! He was being quite shaky but it turned out he was just going off and vomiting because he gets quite nervous.

"He was a real little star though. He reminded me of so many people – a cross between Iggy Pop, Norman Wisdom, I mean there were so many people I saw in him, it was incredible. I've worked with enough people to know when someone's got some personality to play with. And Ricky had it in spades."

"An early list of songs. Note no. 5 'Hail to the Chief' later renamed 'Caroline, Yes' and no.17 the new song 'I Predict a Riot'" NICK

"Potential band names. I did a lot of this" NICK

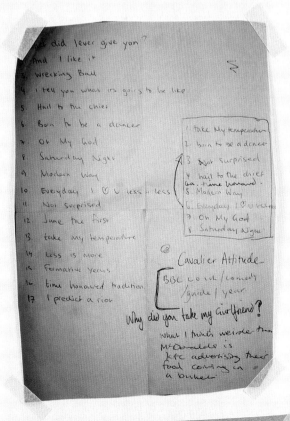

Kaiser Chiefs
Employment B-Unique

We've waited a long time for this, but Blur have finally returned to their roots. After the washed-out experimentalism of 'Think Tank', they've come full-circle back to that which they've always been best at. Pop. Songs. Old friends have returned: long-time producer Stephen Street is back, undoubtedly to recapture some of that 'Parklife' magic and – though things are still tense – they've managed to coax Graham Coxon out of his Camden hole to provide the introductory motorbike revving on hot new track 'Saturday Night'. The album's title, 'Employment', is a cheeky nod to their debut, 'Leisure'. And there's even a track called 'The Modern Way' about – get this! – how British life is rubbish! The boys are back! Now all that's left is to don a Union Jack-emblazoned wife-beater, step outside into glorious sunshine with a warm Stella, and party like it's 1994... Waitaminute: where's that CD case? Kaiser Chiefs? What the fuck? Boy, is our face red.

Sorry Kaisers, it's an all too-easy, criminally convenient place to put you. Kaiser Chiefs aren't Blur, aren't Pulp, aren't XTC, aren't The Specials, aren't... well, you get the picture. Kaiser Chiefs are the Kaiser Chiefs, five Britpop-obsessed, Leeds-based misfits: Ricky Wilson (vocals, electrified skanking), Andrew 'Whitey' White (guitar, the occasional zoot suit), Simon Rix (bass, large curly Afro), Nick 'Peanut' Baines (keyboards, ridiculous pork-pie hats) and Nick Hodgson (drums, the secret

mastermind behind the Chiefs). But let's not go straight to the arse-kissing, there's some rummaging in their dark past to be done. Because the Cheeves aren't fooling us – no sir – we've seen the files, we've found the CD singles in the bargain bin of Woolworths. Apparently, from 2002-2004, there existed a band called Parva consisting of five gentlemen, also from Leeds, coincidentally bearing the same names as the Kaiser Chiefs who, with their workmanlike garage racket, sounded like a slightly hip Six By Seven (if such a thing were possible).

They released three sneering singles that featured lyrics like, *"You're into new self-destruction/Kill all your friends"* and, *"Kill me in my sleep/Cos I'm out of my head/I'm awake in my bed"*. Parva were rubbish. But, praise be. Instead of clinging to the already bursting garage rock bandwagon by their fingernails, Parva wisely decided to let go. Tumbling to the ground, they dusted themselves off and waved goodbye to the likes of Jet and The Datsuns, who refused to move over and give them seats. Yes, they saw the light, and we should be thankful.

One fateful day, ashamed at the soulless copyist attitude that pervaded Parva's sound, they decided to scrap the songs, scrap the moniker, and start afresh. They started on a new name, one nicked from Leeds United defender Lucas Radebe's former South African team, the Kaiser Chiefs. Then came the songs. Hideously catchy, schizoid numbers liberally and unapologetically dressed in the quirkiness and tunefulness of Britpop. But it would be foolish – nay, idiotic – to paint this as a second coming. Tony Blair is still entrenched at Number 10

"oooohhhs" and *"ahhhhhs"* buoyed along by a retarded keyboard pulse lifted from *Tron*. Then there's 'I Predict A Riot', a tale of walking/running through Leeds after pub closing time and avoiding getting your indie ass kicked on the way home, another example of the Kaisers' smiling-though-their-teeth approach. It's a sentiment with which anyone who's been chased down the street by slavering townies just for sporting a dime-sized tear in their jeans, can relate. As those who've been set a-wiggle by its frenetic Saturday-morning cartoon bounce at their local indie discotheque can attest to, it's hardly the most cerebral of anthems and if you picked up 'Employment' expecting a Bloc Party-style level of social awareness, you'd be disappointed. Like The Killers and Franz before them, the Kaiser Chiefs are about crafting the finest pop they can manage without compromising themselves, and do so unashamedly.

That 'I Predict A Riot' segues seamlessly into 'Modern Way' is a testament to the overall standard of 'Employment''s tunes, in that the singles – infectious as they are – manage to slip by almost without notice. Yes, every track here could be a single. Every single one. As befits a band who load their songs with lots of meaningless non-verbal *"oooohhh"*, *"ahhhhs"* and *"ho ho ho hos"*, there's a track called simply, 'Na Na Na Na Naa' – Morrissey they ain't. But unlike labelmates The Ordinary Boys, who revel in bite-sized yob philosophy, the Kaisers are not about stretching themselves beyond their intellectual means. Case in point: 'You Can Have It All', a beautifully ponderous

> ### "The singles – infectious as they are – manage to slip by almost without notice. Because every track here could be a single. Every single one"

but Cool Britannia is most assuredly dead. This is stinking, Rotten Britannia, replete with its flawed intelligence dossiers, mooching asylum seekers and a deluge of rain and pain. There's absolutely nothing to be happy about, right? Wrong!

We've got 'Employment', which along with Bloc Party and The Others, completes a glorious hat-trick of debuts released in the past month. It's yet another wonderful example of Britain's current rock renaissance. Obviously, the hard lessons learnt in Parva have paid off; 'Employment' is a strong record in which you'd be hard-pressed to identify any filler. Opener 'Everyday I Love You Less And Less' sets the tone, with a glut of

song that couldn't care less about what it's saying (and what it's saying is, *"You can have it all/If it's alright"*), and couldn't sound more Beach Boys if Brian Wilson were to come along and dump ten tons of sand into the Kaisers' living room. The Beach Boys parallel extends to closing track 'Caroline, Yes', which drifts along in a similar manner to its distant cousin, 'Pet Sounds' closer 'Caroline, No', albeit with even more vocal harmonies than Wilson and co could muster.

Anyone who finds 'I Predict A Riot''s pithy couplet, *"Walking through town is quite scary/It's not very pretty I tell thee"* galling may have a tough time swallowing the majority of Ricky's lyrics. His word brinksmanship reaches its zenith on 'Time Honoured Tradition' – a staccato, ghost-house ride through a series of ever-so-slightly moralising lessons, such as, *"It's a common misconception, but true without exception/ These nights of booze catch up with youse"*. However, as he brazenly cartwheels through language the instinct is to applaud rather than mock.

In America, where anything to escape these isles and make it across the Atlantic is considered Britpop, the Kaisers are turning heads. 'I Predict A Riot' managed to slip into influencial rock mega-station K-ROQ's Top Ten most-played records. So, British through and through these people may be, but with a record this marvellous you may have to get used to seeing much less of them very soon. **Mike Sterry**

GAINFUL EMPLOYMENT

A track-by-track guide with chief Chiefs Ricky Wilson and Nick Hodgson

Everyday I Love You Less And Less
Nick: "It's kinda new-wavey, kinda fast, very cheese."
Ricky: "It's about a girl but you shouldn't mention her name, as that'd mean she's won."

I Predict A Riot
Nick: "I wrote it on the piano in my mam and dad's house, then took it to rehearsals."
Ricky: "We wrote it purely for Leeds but people in LA, San Francisco, New York and Russia still identity with it."

Modern Way
Nick: "One of our early songs."
Ricky: "When we were less successful, we saw a lot of friends of ours in Leeds getting successful and 'Modern Way' is about that – just wanting it so much that you'll do it."

Na Na Na Na Naa
Ricky: "My favourite song on the album, just because it's a bit stupid. Every now and then, you fancy a McDonald's, so I suppose it's the McDonald's break on our album."

You Can Have It All
Ricky: "That's for our lil'uns. On the first verse, Nick wrote about his girlfriend, on the second verse, I wrote about my girlfriend. I'm not afraid to say I've got a girlfriend, which is refreshing for a boyband."

Oh My God
Nick: "That's the third song we ever wrote."
Ricky: "It's a cracker, innit? It's about being in a band, about being a fish out of water. The first leap's always the hardest."

Born To Be A Dancer
Nick: "It was just another upbeat song with a quirky guitar riff, when we recorded the demo it sounded a bit like something off The Beatles' 'Abbey Road'."

Saturday Night
Nick: "This was the second song we ever wrote. We had just seen the Polysics on TV the night before, and we said, 'Well, let's have a song like them!' but it really didn't turn out that way."

What Did I Ever Give You?
Ricky: "About when you wake up in the morning, and feel guilty and you don't know why."

Time Honoured Tradition
Ricky: "Another fast-food break but it's actually about living healthily. At the speed we're doing stuff,

I don't understand where bands find the time to do drugs."

Caroline, Yes
Ricky: "A nod to The Beach Boys (*Brian Wilson* pictured). Without West Coast guitar music, the Kaisers wouldn't exist."

Team Mate
Ricky: "I wanted a little lullaby at the end to wish people off to sleep. It's quite reflective."

THE INDEPENDENT ON SUNDAY | 24.4.05

ABC
ARTS • BOOKS • CULTURE

SEVEN-DAY TELEVISION AND RADIO GUIDE
PAGES 36-53

ALISON STEADMAN
JOHN MORTIMER
STEPHEN BAYLEY
JOAN BRADY
MARK SIMPSON
SUZI FEAY

KAISER
CHIEFS
On the road with the
hottest band of the year

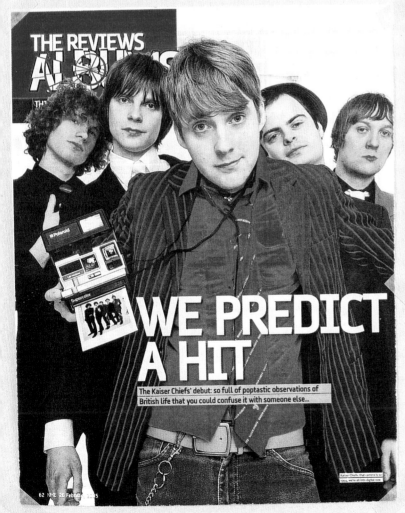

WE PREDICT A HIT

The Kaiser Chiefs' debut: so full of poptastic observations of
British life that you could confuse it with someone else...

Kaiser Chiefs: that camera is so 1994, we're all into digital now

"I used to
wear loads of crap
around my neck.
Very Mr. T.
When I took
it off I felt
much lighter"
RICKY

"I actually once had teeth marks once where I'd got bitten." RICKY

I get a lot of claw marks from people, from when I go into the crowd. I actually had teeth marks once where I'd got bitten. Not in a nasty way, I think it was more that they wanted to consume part of me. But you get a lot of hand marks on your arms and stuff.

"This is a picture of me handing out bread to the starving." Ricky

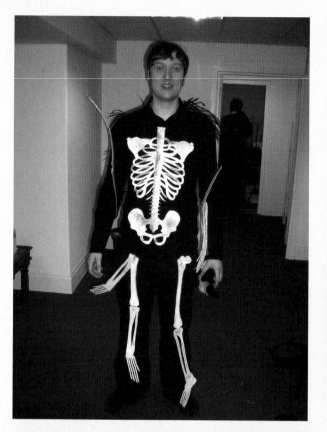

"The skeleton
costumes were
poorly constructed.
You wouldn't
really want one."

Ricky

Legendary director returns to music to flesh out Kaisers clip

Promo focus

Working with The Kaiser Chiefs, legendary promo director Tim Pope has created a promo which can bear comparison with his best work, spanning acts including The Cure and Fatboy Slim.

Opening, in Britpop style, in a good old-fashioned greasy spoon, the promo sees Kaiser keyboardist Nick "Peanut" Baines donning X-ray specs and, upon looking at his bandmates, their skeletal forms jigging away.

Shortly after, frontman Ricky Wilson, falls through a picture which is hanging on the cafe wall into a sort of domestic hell: the front room of his cloying girlfriend, the subject of the song and her equally cloying parents. This scene runs in parallel with the others, creating a sense of looking from one manic world to another.

Pope says the Kaisers wanted the visuals to reflect the way their lyrics deal with the minutiae of everyday life. "I spoke to Ricky, who said the band wanted to start it in a cafe," he says. "As soon as I spoke to the band the idea became flesh in my head. I hung that flesh around the bones of my original idea."

Pope's first idea for the video came from the tiny nugget of a lyric belted out by Ricky Wilson: "I know I feel it in my bones."

"I heard the word 'bones' in the song and jumped on it," says Pope. "There's a famous piece from the early days of animation with dancing skeletons that idea worked very well with the jumpy and frenetic nature of the song."

The promo utilises both hi-tech post-production effects and in-camera effects, something which Pope says he always enjoys. The production also demanded the renting a number of real, live rats – as well as a dead one, which had to be insured for the princely sum of £400.

● A full version of this review features in the May issue of *Promo* magazine, which is published this week. For subscription details, contact David Pagendam on 020 7921 8320.

The gu

Riot act

The Kaiser Chiefs on fighting form

ALL SORTS OF BALLS

These are different balls used in six different sports. Can you say which is used for which particular game?

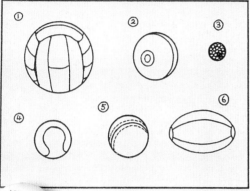

WORLD CUP WILLIE

AGONY & ECSTACY

Separated at birth:
KAISER CHIEFS &
KAISER CHIEFS

Andy Melchior

Six tenuous degrees of separation from
Johannesburg's famed Kaizer Chiefs Football Club
to Kaiser Chiefs the Leeds indie pop band.

1. Soweto born **Lucas Radebe** starts off on the road to becoming South Africa's first real football superstar debuting in 1989 for Kaizer Chiefs FC.
2. In 1994 he gets the opportunity to play abroad when he is bought by Leeds United FC for £250,000.
3. After a successful World Cup in France captaining South Africa he is made club captain at Leeds United for the 1998/99 season earning him the nickname "The Chief".
4. The video for Kaiser Chief's debut single "Oh My God" is shown at half time prior to Radebe coming on for what looks like his final appearance in a Leeds shirt during the last eight minutes of the game.
5. "Lucas Radebe apparently said he would do anything for a band in Leeds called the Kaiser Chiefs," says drummer Nick Hodgson.
6. A week later the entire five-piece is at Leeds United training ground to meet their South African hero. SW

KAISER CHIEFS' DEBUT SINGLE OH MY GOD IS OUT NOW ON DROWNED IN SOUND RECORDINGS. WWW.KAISERCHIEFS.CO.UK.

> "I thought
> footballers
> still wore tight
> shorts but everyone
> laughed at mine,
> including the Leeds
> United players,
> coaches and
> kitchen staff"
> NICK ON TRAINING
> AT ELLAND ROAD

"Simon hopes
that one day
this top will
get him a free
Porsche"
RICKY

"A bird swooped
down and stole
Peanut's cigar"
NICK

"I think I preferred the white scarf"
RICKY

POWER CHOPSTICK FOR WILDCATS

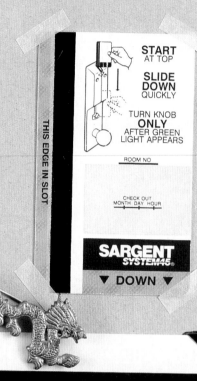

KAISER CHIEFS

THE CRIBS

TOKYO
01.23 /24
LIQUIDROOM

NAGOYA
01.26
NAGOYA CLUB QUATTRO

OSAKA
01.27
BIG CAT

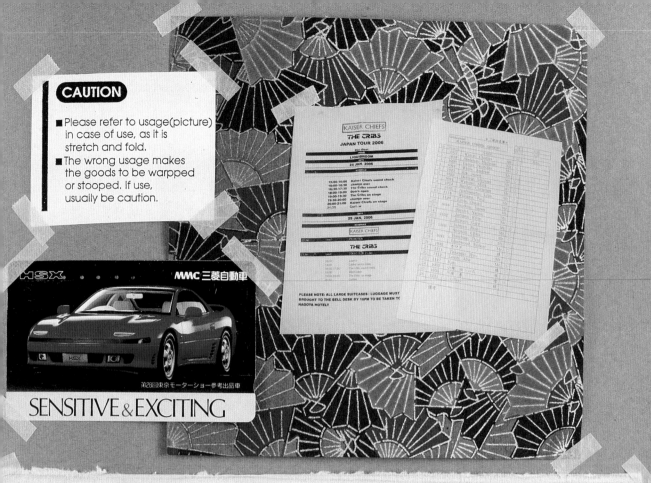

HSX   MMC 三菱自動車

第26回東京モーターショー参考出品車

SENSITIVE & EXCITING

"I remember this was quite funny.
I think it was taken at about nine
minutes past four. Japan time."
RICKY

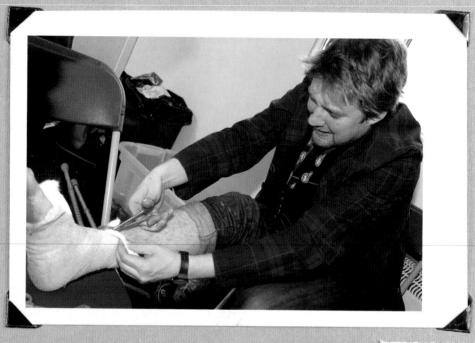

Ricky's Rock Injuries

"I was determined not to look like a pussy in front of Dave Grohl" RICKY

Ricky: The first time I did my leg in was in America. It was in
Seattle at the Crocodile Café, the place owned by one of REM. I
just did a little jump. And I landed on a drum stick. It was a
real comedy fall, I just slipped up and my ankle felt like it was
on fire, like a million red hot sewing needles being pushed into
the bone of the right ankle.

It was more painful the next day but it was actually quite good
for that tour because I got a wheelchair as soon as I got to the
airport, to get wheeled to the aeroplane and then you get a
really good seat with loads of leg room, then you get wheeled off!
I recommend injuring your leg to everyone if they're flying.

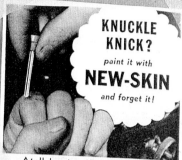

KAISER

KAISER CHIEFS frontman **RICKY WILSON** has his leg in plaster after injuring himself leaping about on stage.

The Leeds rockers' singer was left doubled up. But like a trouper he picked himself up and finished the the gig in Portugal.

Last night a groggy Ricky told me: "We were just three songs in to the set. I was singing Every Day I Love

You Less And Less, jumped in the air and forgot where the floor was.

"I got X-rayed and injected and told to stay in bed for a week.

"There's not much chance of that until January so I've had to put it off."

Ricky spent Tuesday night sweating in a roasting Portuguese hospital with his

GRIEF

"They are all fake injuries. He acts extremely well"
PEANUT

injured right leg in the air. But the X-rays revealed no fractures so doctors put on a plaster cast and gave him the all-clear to carry on the Kaisers' tour — with strict orders to avoid stage diving.

Ricky injured his left ankle earlier this year in a leap from a speaker stack during the band's US Tour, *left*.

Last night a band spokesman said: "Ricky has

torn ankle ligaments. Shows planned for this weekend, Lowlands, Pukkelpop and V Festival, will go ahead.

"But Ricky will be less mobile than usual — and won't be climbing any lighting rigs."

The second time I did my ankle in was in Portugal at a festival. That was weird because the next day in *The Mirror* there was a story explaining that apparently I fell over, was screaming "I'm dying, I'm dying, call me an ambulance now", and the fans were all really worried and crying! What actually happened was, I did it right at the beginning of the show, did the whole set, walked off and went to hospital about four hours later. But the way they made it seem was like I demanded an ambulance to rush me to hospital. I went in the van! I couldn't stop the gig anyway because that was the first time Dave Grohl had watched us and he was stood at the side of the stage. I was determined not to look like a pussy in front of Dave Grohl.

There was one when I was in Japan the first time, when I fell off stage and they didn't really know what to do. I whacked me head on the floor, went straight back and hit my head on the stage.

For about three songs I didn't know what was going on at all. I remembered all the words though! Mick (Webster, co-manager) got some painkillers for me onstage. I'd already had two beers, so I was just gone for the rest of the day. It was quite a pleasant feeling.

> "I've got Dave's number. I text him. He doesn't reply to me. He replies to Peanut!" NICK

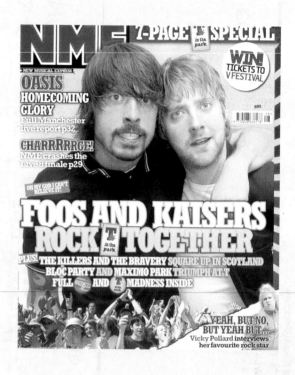

Whitey: Do you wanna ring Dave now? Ring Dave?
Nick: I've got Dave's number. I text him. He doesn't reply to me. He replies to Peanut!
Nick: We did a lot of things with the Foo Fighters. The bowling with them is something we can pick out
Whitey: Dave was actually a very, very good bowler.
Nick: That's why we call him Dave Bowhl. With an H.
Simon: He can bowl, drum, sing and play guitar. Me and Nick played a song in a bar with him one night.
Nick: There were two guys in the bar playing and singing. And a punter came along, and did 'Everlong' and I said to Dave Grohl, go on, you'll make his life, if you go up and he said no. But I kept on at him and he eventually did it, and went up and sang the last couple of lines of 'Everlong' with this guy. And the guy was just in a different world.

Nick: Then someone in the bar asked the Kaiser Chiefs to play a song. It was 'I Predict A Riot'. Simon in the middle playing guitar. Me on Simon's left and Dave on the other side. Both of us singing 'I Predict A Riot' in a crowded bar outside one of the venues, late at night in middle America.
Peanut: He loves that song.
Simon: Foo Fighters had two or three luxurious dressing rooms but they would always come to our box room and hang out.
Nick: I think they liked it 'cos it reminded them of how it used to be.

Happiness is a muddy slit

"Quite simply,
some snaps of us
in America...

SXSW Texas March 2005

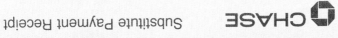

TO ENSURE PROPER POSTING, ALL APPLICABLE FIELDS MUST BE COMPLETED AND PRINTED LEGIBLY. ONE TRANSACTION PER COUPON.

Substitute Payment Receipt   CHASE   The Chase Manhattan Bank

On the set of Letterman.

A wheel chair race at the aiport.

> "... during one
> of our eight
> trips there
> in 2005"
>
> PEANUT

doug weston's
Troubadour
presents
KROD
KAISER
CHIEFS WELCOMES
MORNINGWOOD
MAXIMO
PARK
Tavern

PURCHASE ORDE

TOPS—FORM 3245   LITHO IN U.S.A.

APPLICATION FOR CREDIT

Location of Home Office

THIS BLANK MUST BE FILLED OUT

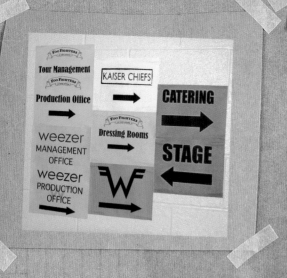

Tour Management
Production Office

KAISER CHIEFS →

CATERING →

weezer
MANAGEMENT
OFFICE

Dressing Rooms →

STAGE ←

weezer
PRODUCTION
OFFICE

W

"I remember having the grump 'cos Si got the same shirt as me"

RICKY

"We're in Berlin and we could have done this a week ago!" RICKY

Simon: We were very insistent we wanted to do the 'Help' album. But it took us to the very last second to find a song because no one would give us clearance on anything. You'd think that people would give you clearance on charity records, wouldn't you?

Ricky: Name and shame them!

Simon: The Beatles. And when they said no we asked The Who if we could do 'Can't Explain'. It didn't matter in the end though, what we did was really good.

Ricky: Nick was in a shop called Retro Boutique on Hyde Park Corner (if you're ever in there, say hello to my pal, Morris) and The Slits' version of 'I Heard It Through The Bassline' was on. We had a day until we were going to Berlin for a show and were recording it in a studio there.

Simon: The most stressful thing was we thought everyone was doing it in a day and when we talked to Cenzo (Townsend), who was engineering our track, and asked him what he'd been up to, he said, "I was recording Razorlight for the 'Help' album yesterday!"

Ricky: I was like, isn't it all getting done today!?! We're in Berlin and we could have done this a week ago!

Simon: We wanted to make it a dance floor classic. It didn't really work. One person said, "I quite like it but you didn't really take it very far." Where do you want us to take it?

Ricky: We took it to Berlin and back.

N'S ATTIRE
o.uk
Everything is Brilliant
IN LEEDS
2-WAY CUFFS
These can be turned and used a second time
ENJOYMENT:
AVAILABLE AS A DVD
OR ON 7500 COLOUR
SOUVENIR SLIDES
Everything is Brilliant
AT
ENJOYMENT CONTAINS
THESE FIVE HIT SINGLETS

Legendary Leeds drinking album.

Sing-a-long Kaisers with
Peanut and vocals.

Original German language adaptation.

Volume 2.

Original solo career bid.

Light orchestral Kaiser songs
performed by Mr. & Mrs. Peanut.

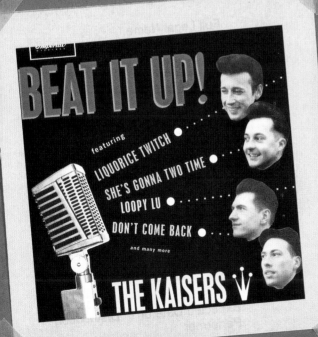

In-store signing of fans'
albums. 2005

"I knew we had finally made it when Whitey got a plectrum holder. Actually, I knew we had made it when he got a spare plectrum." RICKY

"Somewhere along the line tickets got printed and then they're on sale in shops. The tickets said 'Kaiser Chiefs' secret gig'" SIMON

Leeds Cockpit June 2005

Ricky: Yeah, it's one of those gigs where everyone says they
were there, but if you counted them it wouldn't add up!

Simon: Yeah, we wanted just to do a secret gig and somewhere
along the line tickets got printed and then they're on sale in
shops. The tickets said 'Kaiser Chiefs' secret gig'. *(Laughs)*

Simon: It was a really good idea doing a small gig 'cos we thought
it would be a bit crazy and all that, which it was. We were
playing on the smallest stage we had done for a long time. Ricky
just ran out and immediately jumped in the crowd. I was having
a great time apart from that there was a camera woman and I kept
hitting her around the head with my bass. I don't like to
hit ladies.

Ricky: We learnt our lesson - you can't keep secrets in Leeds.
Especially when you get tickets printed. (Laughs)

A BIG LIFE

"What's this guy taking a picture of? He's crap!" RICKY

"This is a
picture of Whitey's
scooter helmet"
Simon

OOH!
THEY'VE GONE ALL BIG!
KAISER CHIEFS
THEIR AMAZING STORIES FROM LIVE8, GLASTO AND MORE

FRANZ IN
PRIVATE JETS
WHITE STRIPES BACK
TO BASICS IN CALIFORNIA

"It's not just about indie!"
HARD-FI SOUND OFF
Plus... lord save us,
here comes acid folk

Glastonbury, 24 June 2005

"I don't want to see the stage until I walk on it. If I see a band on it, that's when I get nervous".

Ricky: The one thing I haven't done is see the Pyramid Stage yet. I'd like to see The Killers tonight but I don't want to see the stage until I walk on it. If I see a band on it, that's when I get nervous, and you're throwing up for half an hour before a gig. People have been asking me what I'm going to say but I don't want to think about it. You can really tell when bands have worked it out before-hand. So I'm just trying to empty my head of it and just hope someone pushes me on at 2.55 tomorrow.

Hail to the Kaiser Chiefs
On the road with this year's Glastonbury heroes

Jeremy Vine's secrets • The unseen Sixties • Mark Hix's summer berries • Anna Pavord

Printed in Great Britain by Blackie & Son Ltd, Glasgow

Whitey: Whoa! Glastonbury, the big one eh?

Nick: We were there the whole weekend. I'd never been before because I always said I'll only ever go when we play.

Whitey: (Thumps table) No, I said that!

Nick: I said it as well! I've been saying it for 10 years!

Whitey: But then I went!

Nick: It wasn't me being all bravado. I only wanted to go when I had to. Because if you're just in a tent it would be a bloody nightmare! It would be a disaster!

"GLASTOFIVE"

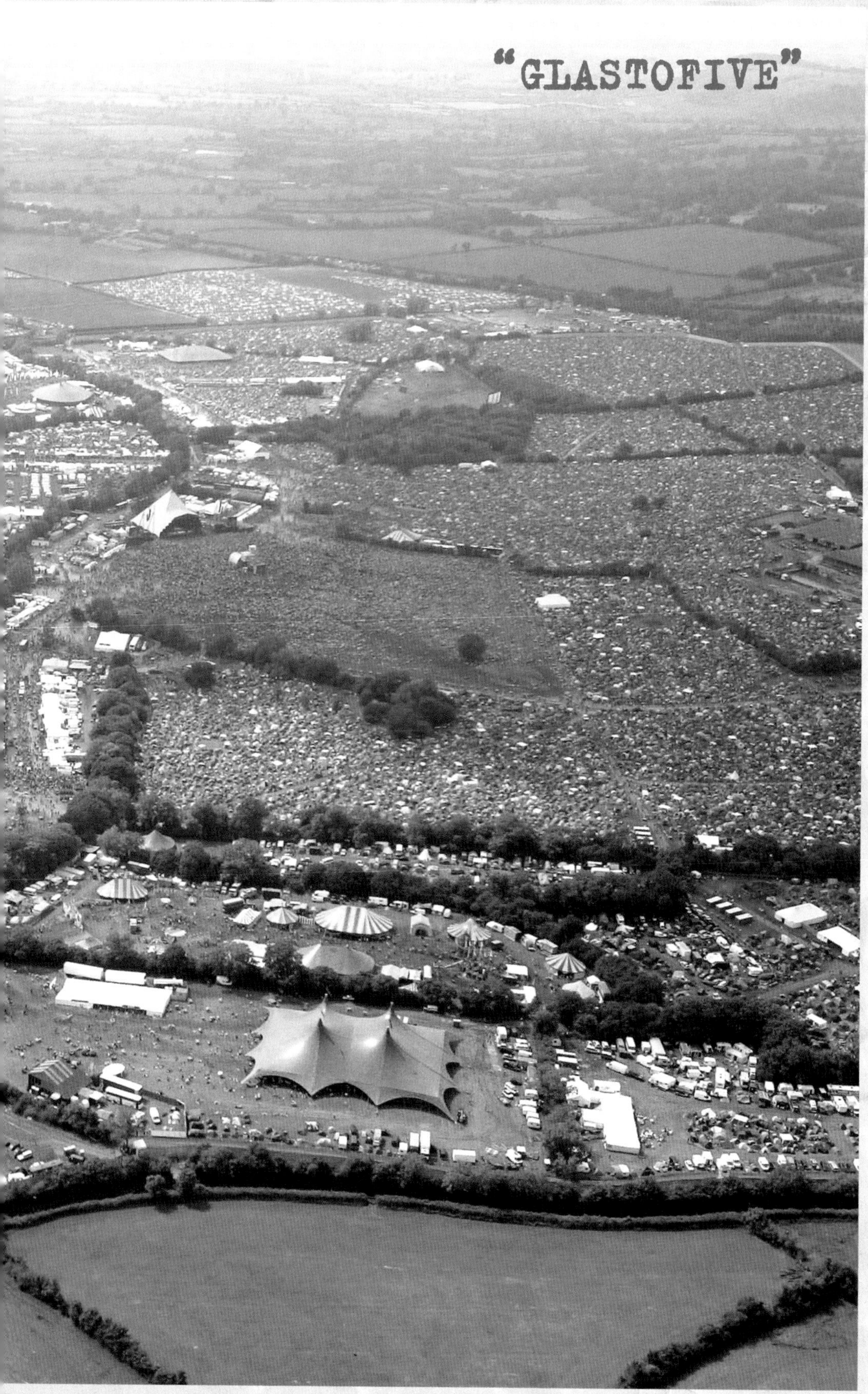

"Our Glastonbury
backdrop cost us
loads of money
and we only got to
use it once"
NICK

#2 KAISER CHIEFS' RICKY WILSON

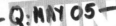
— Q: MAY 05 —

I hear you're playing on the Main Stage on Saturday at Glastonbury. Looking forward to it?
"Immensely. I've never really been before. Quite arrogantly, I always said I'd never go until we were playing there. That was eight years ago. I always watch it on the telly, though."

Who will you be watching?
"My girlfriend really wants to see Coldplay, so I'll have to be there to hold her hand."

Care to make a prediction about the weather?
"It's going to be hot, hot, hot. I'm a perpetual optimist."

Complete the following sentence: this year I'll be...
"...not planning a thing. The worst thing is being stuck with someone who's got an agenda for the day – it's a nightmare."

"**I'm literally getting chills thinking about 'cos I knew it was good**" NICK

James Sandom (manager): I associate 'Oh My God' with so many great memories. At Glastonbury with 60,000+ singing it back and a green inflatable dinosaur on stage was honestly one of the proudest moments of my life. I had this real inner feeling of pride that I think I've only ever felt on my wedding night other than on that day.

Ricky: That was the turning point for me anyway, but I think it was a turning point for us as a band too. I think we'd proved ourselves as a proper rock band. We're not an 'art rock' band; we're not flim-flam, we've proved to a lot of people that we're actually major contenders and are going to be around for a long time.

James Sandom: Glastonbury was the moment the band were no longer contenders. They were leaders. To say the band turned in a blinder is an understatement, they stole it... it was astonishing and I believe paved the way for much that followed.

Nick: I'm literally getting chills thinking about it now 'cos I knew it was good.

Glastonbury, Saturday 25 June 2005

Ricky: Because usually I'm sick before we go on stage, people just know not to come and talk to me. But this time I was jumping up and down and like 'This is gonna be ACE!' And it was.

Whitey: I wasn't really nervous, more apprehensive.

Nick: I'm always nervous at festivals 'cos we never get a soundcheck. I came on. Sat down. And there was NOTHING at all. Muted. So I had to sing the first song without being able to hear the rest of the band. And I just thought to myself — shit. And I was resigned to the fact this is my Glastonbury. But they came on for the second song!

Ricky: I don't know whether it was because I was really hungover and just didn't care, but I was just performing on stage at Glastonbury, as opposed to being nervous, I was just really excited, and it was the first time I've ever done that before.

Michael Eavis (Glastonbury God): We gave them that good slot, the Saturday spot and of course they completely surprised everyone, they really delivered the goods, didn't they?

'The Radio 1 presenter
Jo Whiley was stood on a
balcony at the side of
the stage. I saw right up
her skirt as we went on.'
RICKY

Live 8 in Philadelphia, July 2005

"I almost stole the Fresh Prince's thunder!" RICKY

Ricky: We set off from Leeds at 7am the day before and arrived in Philadelphia at about 9 in the evening, so our body clocks were a bit messed up. Then in the morning we had to get up really early because we were told we had to be there before people started filling the streets — although it turned out we were the only band that did that. Everyone swanned in later in blacked-out people carriers — we came in a taxi!

For the first few hours my nerves kicked in. We were first on, so a lot of people were asking me what I was going to say. Bob Geldof is the patron saint of getting a point across, I don't know if you need the guy from the Kaiser Chiefs saying anything.

The gig itself was incredible. We were the first people in America to do Live 8. I remember starting it by saying, "Ladies and gentlemen of the world, welcome to Live 8". I felt like an alien invader addressing the planet. Will Smith was on after us and he said almost exactly the same as me. I almost stole the Fresh Prince's thunder!

We opened with 'I Predict A Riot', which with a million people watching in the heat, all raring to go probably wasn't the best idea (*laughs*) but they seemed to like it. The funniest thing of all to me, though, was the only time we played Philadelphia before, we played in front of 19 people. This time it was nearer 3 billion! If it goes up at that rate we'll be alright.

When we came off stage, Black Eyed Peas were about to go on. We'd opened a bottle of champagne and I was sharing it with Fergie — clang! namedrop — and I was in a funny mood. I said to her, "A lot of people say you look like my girlfriend," and she went, "Oh, that's a nice thing to say". I looked at her and said, "No, not really". Then she was pulled off to go on stage with this mortified look on her face — what just happened then?! I didn't mean it like that but it came across really badly.

Daily Star
June 10 '05

"This wasn't part of the performance at Live 8.
    This is behind the scenes" Nick

"Peanut taking a break from his role as chief chair straightener at Live 8" NICK

'As usual, we were first to arrive. Will Smith took this photo"

Peanut

The highlight of my day was standing out front watching Stevie Wonder, and seeing on the big screens a shot of where we were by the side of the stage. On two massive screens, with 5 million people watching in Philadelphia, everyone could see Paula Abdul dancing, going crazy. But stood behind her, nodding his head, was Peanut! He was just going, "Hmm, Cool". It's the funniest thing I've seen in my life!

We all got to meet Paula afterwards, she was ace. And I met Richard Gere too, he said we did a good job. It was odd actually. When I was backstage with all these movie stars I kept feeling that someone would realise they could throw me out at any minute and I wouldn't even have argued, I'd have put my hand up and said, "You're right, I really shouldn't be here". It was a really strange day.

Actually that's what I liked about the Live 8 thing. You had Jay Z, Kaiser Chiefs, Def Leppard, Stevie Wonder – all these things that were totally different, and still a million and a half people came out on the streets to watch it, just because they knew they had to be there for a reason, for the cause. People suddenly realising they have power – it was like a revolution!

We met the mayor of Philadelphia who said to me "You were fantastic, I hope in twenty years' time you come back and headline", but I thought the point is that there should never have to be a Live Aid again – it was a really good party and everything but we don't want another.

"Somebody thought we were a rap act" RICKY

Simon: I only remember a few things. I remember it being quite good and it feeling like quite a momentous thing to be at, but the crowd were miles away. Also, we were doing a load of promo as you do at these events and we got very giddy. We decided we were going to take over the BBC. So we went over, Ricky took the camera off the camera man, and then me and Nick were just talking. Eventually we realised that we were going to interview Graham Norton, so we got him in and interviewed him a bit.

Ricky: I had the camera and I was zooming in and out shouting, "It's just like Going Live!"

Simon: And then it got shown on national television in England! You just think, what am I paying my licence fee for?!

Ricky: Thing is, I think we were supposed to play Hyde Park and then somebody thought we were a rap act — Kaiser. We were told the week before that we were playing Hyde Park. And when they announced it we were like, "They've got it wrong! They've put us on in Philadelphia!" And everyone goes on about how we opened Live 8 — the television broadcast of Live 8 in America started the moment we came off stage! But we got broadcast in England in Hyde Park.

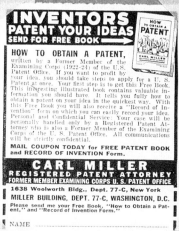

"Peanut did an excellent jo[b]

"Testing, Testing 1. 2. 3. Are the cameras on yet? NO!" RICKY

"What do you mean 'we've started?!'" PEANUT

Ryan Jarman — The Cribs

"We'd heard of the Kaisers a few times — we heard a band from Leeds had got signed but we'd never seen them. Anyway, we were doing a gig at The Cockpit in Leeds just after we'd been signed and they were there.

"Simon knew who we were and said, 'D'ya wanna do a gig together? We're in a band called Kaiser Chiefs.' I said, 'Yeah, cool' and gave him my phone number. But nowt came of it to begin with.

"After that I started to see them out on the town. I used to see Ricky serving behind the bar at this club night called The Village Green. I got to know him, we used to sit and talk about what his band were getting up to. Ricky used to sort us out free pints all the time so I used to think he was a good guy. That was probably 21 months ago he stopped serving there and look at him now, y'know?

"They mainly used to play The Beatles, The Kinks, Blur and stuff like that at The Village Green. I can't remember which Blur song it was they used to play at the end of every night but Nick and that lot used to dance to it. So looking back, the music played at The Village Green was a little bit of a blueprint for the Kaisers. We only ever did a few gigs together back then.

"Their career took off really quickly. There was never any competition involved between us mind, and we've always stayed really good mates. The first time we supported them they'd just completed a tour with The Ordinary Boys and they had three gigs coming up so we supported them on that. We're all really appreciative of being out on the road, because it was not long ago that we were talking about how cool it would be."

"Ricky used to sort us
out free pints all the
time so I used to think
he was a good guy"
RYAN JARMAN

My birthday is the same as Ryan and Gary's so we
all celebrated somewhere in the world" NICK

"I believe that in
20 years time, the above
photo will be on every
music fan's wall as the
most important moment
in band history. (That's
me at the back)"
RICKY

50P

688

50P

687

50P

"Peanut gets ready for his stage performance as Simon removes a shoe to throw at him"

RICKY

Touring with U2

Nick: Did we get the Bono talk? I've been asked this before! It's weird that people call it the Bono talk. I've just realised.

Whitey: No, we didn't.

Nick: Yeah we did! We talked to him, and we were telling him about how we'd been inspired by them.

Whitey: Well he came in and said hello and that.

Nick: He asked us if we were enjoying the gigs and we said yes, we love playing these big venues. And he goes, "That's good, 'cos a lot of bands don't get that buzz, you've obviously got the buzz."

I consider that to be the Bono talk. He's a proper Catholic 'cos when he left he squeezed me shoulder and he shakes hands with two hands. The hand sandwich.

Whitey: Then him and the Edge left in a waft of very nice smells. He did smell very good. As if they don't do gigs, they just walk around smelling good.

Nick: Y'know what Whitey said at the time? He said "They smelt really rich". They _are_ rich people and they're clean.

Ricky: And Adam Clayton has very soft marshmallowy hands.

U2//
VERTIGO//2005
TOUR

Madrid

Thursday, August 11, 2005

Soundcheck	NONE
Doors	5:30 pm
Kaiser Chiefs	7.15 pm
Set Change	8.00 pm
Franz Ferdinand	8.30 pm
Set Change	9.05 pm
U2	9.45 pm
Sunset	9.23 pm
Curfew	midnight

Rick felt unsure that the White-Shoe tent was of any benefit to him.

On tour, U2 like to employ their support acts as stage hands.

No he's not.

Yes he is

SIMON OCT 16TH DSC01128.JPG

Nick with his greatest fan.

That Bono talk.

Kaiser Chiefs
Enjoyment **9**

Tour

Better value is Frai...

...and a bit of *Enjoyment*

...or Green Day's
...is being a
...by there being
...d album.

Kaiser Chiefs don't even have a second album yet, but that doesn't stop their *Enjoyment* (geddit?) package being the pick of the bunch by a long chalk. This has been their year, and there's barely a scene missed. Two full shows from Leeds and San Francisco are in the extras segment, but the main attraction is the 90-minute longform movie, packed with live tracks, all the videos, and cameos from Roger Daltrey, The Cribs, Damon Albarn, Mark Lamarr and, er, Steve Wright. Clips of the band as seven-year-olds and pensioners feature in a documentary charting Ricky's descent into country solo hell, Simon Rix's secluded life as a gardener who thinks he's a romantic poet and Peanut's serene dotage in

California as well as the last known sighting of reclusive guitarist Whitey, in 2008.
It won't convert the people who are concerned that the Chiefs' relentless chirpiness is undermining their music. But it's the only one of this week's bunch to pack the same imaginative punch as *Bullet In A Bible* and also the only one to have the band's fingerprints all over it. Love and good times radiate from every frame of *Enjoyment*, but more than anything, it's a fitting reminder of what a breath of fresh air Kaiser Chiefs have been this year.
It also offers the *second* (and hopefully last) chance you'll get this year to get your very own *NME* journo in your Christmas stocking (the first being some demented hack who outwitted security to get onstage for the climax of Live8). Be afraid. **Dan Martin**

"It just saps the life out of any gig watching a film of it" RICKY

Ricky: We thought about doing a DVD with the express reason of it being a Christmas gift. When you look at our contemporaries' DVDs, they're a live gig, usually outside with loads of fans there. There's huge sweeping camera moments and no matter how much you try to dress it up and make it look expensive it's just extremely boring. It just saps the life out of any gig watching a film of it. Even if you were at the gig and you wanted to spot yourself in the crowd it would still be boring. So we wanted some live stuff but we wanted more than that. We wanted the videos on it, and backstage stuff we've been filming all year.

It used to be important for bands, getting across who you are. A lot of bands recently have been so guarded about revealing their personalities or being honest about who they are. All you get is the record and a few guarded interviews. I think we're a bit different to that. The Beatles did it and if it's good enough for them it's good enough us. People have been calling it a film and it's not, it's just a bit of nonsense!

Hall to prepare for their annual   is no emergency number   now on."
Christmas fair at 8.30am on Saturday.   notice at the hall," he said.

Celebrity scoop for young reporters

THE Bungay High School newspaper landed a remarkable coup with an exclusive interview with members of top band The Kaiser Chiefs.

Fifteen-year-old Grace Harvey, a member of the production team, managed to get a personal chat with both lead singer Ricky Wilson and keyboard player Nick (Peanuts) Baines, pictured, when they were in Southwold on Wednesday for the launch of their new DVD, Enjoyment, at the Electric Picture Palace.

She asked them about their music, their favourite album tracks and their plans for the future — and then joined them in the cinema to watch part of the 90-minute DVD, written and directed by Cally Callomon, from Walpole. Members of the Halesworth based Circle '67 appear in the film.

Grace, who lives in St John's Road, Bungay: "They were really good and helpful and really friendly. It was lovely to have the chance to meet them like that."

Picture: TERRY REEVE

Beccles & Bungay Journal

'DIFFERENT': Kaiser Chiefs members Nick 'Peanut' Baines , centre left, and Ricky Wilson, centre, at the premiere of their DVD Enjoyment in Southwold. Above: Nick with fans Polly Bowman, left, and Grace Harvey   Photos: SIMON PARKER

Seaside launch of rising stars' DVD

East Anglian Daily Times, Thursday, November 24, 2005 www.eadt.co.uk

ONE of the country's top rock acts failed to start a riot when they held the premiere of their new DVD at a Suffolk seaside town yesterday.

A year ago the Leeds-based band the Kaiser Chiefs were virtually unknown but ever since the hit single *I Predict A Riot* was released they have gained fans all over the world.

Their album *Employment* has become a multi-platinum success and the band proved a huge hit at this year's Glastonbury and V festivals.

A DVD charting the band's rise to fame has been produced by Suffolk-based director "Cally" Collomon and yesterday the 90-minute feature was given its premiere at the Electric Picture Palace cinema at Southwold.

On a bitterly cold afternoon only a handful of fans waited outside the art deco cinema to see band members Nick "Peanut" Baines and Ricky Wilson turn up for the private viewing of the DVD.

Lead singer Ricky and keyboard player Peanut happily chatted to their fans, signed autographs, and posed for photographs before going into the cinema.

"This is the first time I

have ever been to Southwold but it is a really nice place. I have enjoyed looking at the shops and tasting the local beer," said Ricky.

Peanut said they had travelled down from Leeds for the premiere and was delighted that it was being held in Southwold.

"Premieres of music DVDs in London happen all the time and we like to be different so here we are in Southwold. There is a strong Suffolk connection with the DVD so this is the place to be," he said.

Cally Collomon lives at Walpole, near Halesworth, and he wrote and directed the DVD that features spoof scenes of the band members as young children talking about their ambitions and as much older men reflecting on their time in the limelight.

Members of the Halesworth-based Circle 67 drama group were chosen to play the part of the band members in their later years.

Mr Collomon said: "Local amateur actors were used as well as one Bill Nighy, who lives down the road from me in Suffolk and is handy with a mic.

"Bill got the point from the off and he also happens to be a knowledgeable fan of Kaiser Chiefs' brand of lunacy." The DVD is called *Enjoyment* and goes on sale from Monday.

Deborah Egan and Claire Smith, of Lowestoft, had travelled all over the country to see the band perform so were not going to miss seeing them at Southwold.

"I really love their music and this was too good an opportunity to miss," said Deborah.

> "No one's ever really been half way through an album and decided to release a new song"
>
> RICKY

Looking Good,
Sounding Better
Do we look bothered?

Record of the Week
I Predict A Riot
Kaiser Chiefs
B-Unique/Polydor

...es of the album having just gone through the 500,000 mark in the UK the
...ment ...osition as the breakthrough band of 2005.
...riends at B-Unique and Supervision management on their
...ct the album to reach the million mark by the end of the
...r gold disc!

A30

'Sink That Ship', August 2005

"It's a bit stupid, I know, but we're a bit stupid" RICKY

Ricky: We'd been working on some new stuff on the road and that was one we really liked. We recorded it, we liked it, so we thought well let's release it. I'm sure there were loads of people ripping their hair out - well the two guys that run our label probably were at the time - going "this is such a stupid idea". But as we were sticking 'I Predict A Riot' out again we wanted to do something new as well and show people where we were going.

I thought we'd get more shit for putting it out again, but the way I saw it, it hadn't really fulfilled its potential, and last summer we played it at festivals and people seemed to like it. The only reason to release singles is to hear them on the radio - you don't make any money from them - and I just wanted to hear it a lot more.

It's about taking risks, do it if you want to do it - don't let anyone tell you not to! We recorded it in a couple of days after Glastonbury, it was supposed to be time off, but it was fun. A lot of bands complain about recording - "We were up all night getting it right, we scrapped everything and we sacked the producer" - but for us it's just a load of fun. We get to play loud and muck around. Not enough of that goes on, record it release it, record it release it - don't wait around.

No one's ever really been half way through an album and decided to release a new song that's not on it. It's a bit stupid, I know, but we're a bit stupid.

The single will probably be the only place people will ever be able to get 'Sink That Ship' - 'til we do our double A-sides album (laughs). It's not going to be on the next album.

"My parents don't call me Peanut"

Peanut: I got the nickname at school when I was ten years old. We had to draw pictures of ourselves for the new school year. You had to have your photograph taken, write something and draw a picture of yourself. And I drew this picture and my head looked like a peanut. Art was never my thing, unfortunately.

I actually threw the picture away. But some kid was rooting through a bin, as kids do, found it and was like, "Oh look! Peanut head!" and that was it. It just became my nickname.

The whole PFC (Peanut Fan Club) probably started with some chanting when we supported The Ordinary Boys on tour, I reckon. The chants of "Peanut! Peanut!" from the crowd.

Why me? I don't know why. I think it's because I've got a nickname and people like it for some reason.

My parents don't call me Peanut. I did catch my mum out once though. We were at the Leeds Town Hall show (October 2005) and I heard her talking to someone else and referring to me as Peanut, not Nick. I pulled her up on that one.

I don't know if David Bailey did say I was cooler than Charlie Watts. People tell me that but I didn't hear it. I'd like to say yes but I'd be lying.

Manchester mishap, October 2005

"Not a very smooth start" SIMON

Simon: I remember the first night at Manchester Apollo being fraught as we were stood waiting to go on stage, the first time we used the pre-gig film. It was on but there was no sound, then the sound came on extremely loud, then off. So we went on stage behind a curtain (we thought) for our big entrance, only to find that the crowd could see us and the film had to start again, so we had to stand there whilst the entire thing ran again! Not a very smooth start.

Peanut: It was just before the big reveal at the start of the show, you know the bit when the big curtain came down and Dire Straits started?

Peanut: The stage isn't very big so we had literally a few metres between Nick's drum riser and the front of the stage.

Some of the lights were sticking out a bit. So Dire Straits is playing and we've got to walk on and look cool and there's this silhouette of someone stumbling and screaming 'fucking light!'

Nick: A giant silhouette!

Whitey: I banged into a light, stumbled and doubled over! I were bleeding through the gig!

Nick: However, unlike any other situation where you're able to recover, literally the curtain was about to come down and 2,000 people are about to see you.

Leeds homecoming

"It's hard to rock out when you see the family looking on." Whitey

Simon: Half the Leeds team came to one of the gigs. If I check my phone book, under G you might find Gary Kelly.

Whitey: Mine's under K. That was quite good, seeing half of Leeds United jump up and down.

Simon: I remember playing. Trying to look reasonably cool. And I see me mum and dad dancing on the balcony.

Whitey: It's hard to rock out when you see the family looking on. Or you see Peanut's dad in the moshpit. He's been in the moshpit numerous times.

Glasgow, October 2005

Peanut: My dad and his friend had come up to see the show. 'Modern Way' was the next song — I'm down the front about to do my clapping bit and looking up to my left I see my dad on the balcony. The oldest person there by a bit and having a great time... not the first time I've seen him at a gig though. On the April 2005 tour he was spotted in the pit at the Leeds Met show. The rest of the family were safely up on the balcony but he was loving it down there with all the kids, jumping around.

"Looks like I'm writing some super cool lyrics or something else totally cool" RICKY

"We'd try to get The Cribs on stage as often as possible to do 'Modern Way' with us" NICK

X This is to certify
...Peanut...
has acheived the standard of
basic presenter
date: 6/2/05
signed ....
X

xpressradio.co.uk

"The best thing about
doing radio interviews
is meeting your heroes.
Jonny Walker is one.
Mark Goodier is another"
NICK

"I like being on the
radio 'cos 98% of the
time I look 98% shit
so it suits me".
RICKY

Bottom line: Jarvis Cocker confronted Michael Jackson at t...

EDP Feb 16 06

HAT-TRICK: Kaiser Chiefs collect one of their three awards. Right: Katherine Jenkins arrives for the Brits ceremony.

Brits predict a trio for Kaiser Chiefs

I predict another Brit

ONLY a day to go until the Brit awards, which are always a hoot. Who could forget Chumbawamba soaking John Prescott or Justin Timberlake groping Kylie Minogue or the great Jarvis Cocker waggling his bum at Michael Jackson?

I read at the weekend that Charles Kennedy "has attended the event every year since becoming an MP in 1983". I also learned that the 3,900 guests tomorrow will be served 40,000 bottles of wine and 50,000 bottles of beer. Do the maths.

The phrase "I predict a riot" is inescapable. Does that explain why no politicians have been invited this year?

"We're pretty bad at acceptance speeches" NICK

THE SUN: Jan 11 06

I predict a rout

THE KAISER CHIEFS and JAMES BLUNT are in pole position for the Brit Awards after they received the most nominations.

KAISER CHIEFS AND BLUNT UP FOR 5 BRITS EACH

Former Army captain James and the Leeds rockers, whose hits include I Predict A Riot, each scooped five at last night's big launch party.

But while the champagne was flowing for them, **SUGABABES** and **GOLDFRAPP** will be cursing organisers after both suffered unexpected snubs.

I thought the Sugas would have been a dead cert for Best Pop but they picked up only one nomination, for Best Single.

And if the opinion of **MADONNA** means anything, Goldfrapp's Supernature was the best album of 2005.

But hats off to James Blunt.

Many record industry insiders have viewed him as James **BLAND** — commercially successful despite being uncool. But organisers could not ignore more than two million sales of debut album Back To Bedlam — which made it the best selling LP of 2005.

He is going head to head with the Kaisers, right, in two categories — Best Album and Breakthrough.

James is also up for Best Male, Best Single and Best Pop.

The Kaisers, whose album Employment was the fourth-best seller of 2005, are also up for awards for Best Group, Best Rock and Best Live.

Split

But nominations do not always guarantee gongs — just ask **CRAIG DAVID**.

He was nominated for six awards in 2001 and trudged off with nothing.

The Kaisers and posh man of pop James also face the danger of a possible split vote.

If an artist features only in one category they are more likely to receive a large share of the vote.

But if they are nominated in several, voters may be tempted to opt for an underdog in each one. The most interesting battle at the awards, at London's Earls Court on February 15, will be the fiercely competitive Album and Group categories.

GORILLAZ and **COLDPLAY** will be fighting it out for the honours here.

DAMON ALBARN's cartoon collective have had an astonishing year with Demon Days flying off shop shelves. But I reckon that Coldplay just about edge it.

CHRIS MARTIN and Co's third studio album, X&Y, has sold more than five million copies worldwide.

Scottish artists were also toasting success at last night's Brits launch party at the Riverside studios in Hammersmith, West London — **KT TUNSTALL** and **FRANZ FERDINAND** landed three nominations each.

As I revealed on Monday, **ROBBIE WILLIAMS** will also be licking his wounds as he got only one nomination, in the Best Male category.

And I told you yesterday how **OASIS** were miffed at being left out of the running in Best Album and Best Band.

Robbie can always console himself in the knowledge that he still holds the record for the most Brit wins — 14, including three with **TAKE THAT.**

But you can bet he'd swap a few CD sales for the Best Album gong this year.

"I'm gonna stick a toilet roll on the NME Award, see how it looks" NICK

The Kaisers win three Brits (Best British Rock Act, Best British Live Act and Best British Group) and an NME Award (Best Album 'Employment').

Ricky: I can't remember much of the Brits. What I do remember is we were the first to arrive. We always do this! Whenever people say "You need to be there at 10 a.m.", we're there at 10 a.m. We've realised now most people in bands ignore these rules and just turn up whenever. We were there from 10 a.m. and we didn't even get to eat!

Nick: My favourite memory of the Brits was probably playing. I was quite nervous but I really enjoyed it. Normally when we do TV it's never the best performance and I rarely get into it 'cos it goes too quickly, but this time I actually got into it. I'm not bothered about awards, in general. Although I do have the NME Award in my flat at the moment. The Brits are still at the engravers'. I've got the NME Award in my hand now. I'm gonna stick a toilet roll on it see how it looks. (*Pauses.*) It looks crap. That was Ricky's idea. I might use it as a door stop. I think if you're doing something really kind of blasé with it yet dead cool. Like use a Brit to keep your door open. (*Pauses.*) I tried it as a door stop then it didn't really work. I like my old door stop.

Ricky: I'm glad we didn't win that many NME Awards. Because we had this stupid table right at the front and I was just in a weird mood. I thought we were gonna get booed or something. But when Peter Hook said "Shall we give Franz's award to the Kaiser Chiefs?" there was a huge cheer! And it made me think, "They don't hate us!" It meant a lot to me to have the whole indie fraternity cheering us.

Nick: I really enjoyed the NME Awards. I was kind of dreading it because of all the nominations. But none of us wanted to win more than one because we didn't want to keep getting up onstage and annoying everyone. It was good that we won one, and best album was perfect. In the paper the next day it said: "The big losers of the night were the Kaiser Chiefs". How can we be the big losers — we've won! And we were nominated for six! The voting public were obviously interested, so the bigger loser on the night was a band that didn't get nominated at all.

Ricky: I'll look back fondly on a lot of these things in years to come. But right now I'm just concentrating on making the next record and I don't give a shit. I'm not saying I didn't wanna win, it's just there are more important things to us than awards ceremonies right now. Like the second album.

, Peanut & Whitey got
rds. I got champagne.
Ricky got Madonna.
Best Tombola ever!"
SIMON

Postscript, summer 2006

"But how do you spell learnt?" NICK

Ricky: We've got lots of bits and bobs. I've got a little black book full of my ideas, and late last year I bought Nick one too. I don't know if he's been using it. I'm really looking forward to it. Working on the second album is as exciting if not more than the last one. We go in for three days a week, do five or six hours at a time. At the moment, it's just like the old days.

I think the big difference between then and now is that then we were trying to write some songs for people to just either notice or to like, so at the end of the gig they might remember us. Whereas now we write songs and you kind of know there's an audience, you're getting excited, thinking yes, people are going to really like that song.

Ricky: When we first started, we were always first on of three bands and you've really go to just put all your cards on the table and play. I mean with only five or six songs, you've really got to just punch them in the face. Not literally but musically. And now it's kind of weird because we're making music that people are already very interested in hearing.

Simon: I think one of the things we've learnt from writing 'Employment', is that even now we'll be in rehearsal and jam or we play something and it's got to be new and different and also be us, to be a good Kaiser Chiefs song. For ages Nick had a song which sounded like a brilliant Neil Young song

Ricky: Perfect for The Thrills. He's actually trying to sell it to them at the moment.

Nick: 'Heat Dies Down' is one of the new songs. 'Learnt My Lesson Well' is another one. I'll be pleased to see them in the print. But how do you spell learnt? Is it 'N T' or is it 'E D'? Learnt or Learned?

"It's almost like we don't have to reinvent ourselves, we're just happy to let it grow the way it's growing"

Peanut

Nick: Whatever's grammatically correct. I think learned is grammatically incorrect.

Peanut: Well you sing though that I've learnt, you said that I've learnt my lesson well.

Nick: Anyway, these songs are better. They are the next step up. More developed.

Simon: Someone said they're more grown up than 'Employment' which I didn't like.

Nick: My brother said that.

Simon: Mark and Martin (from the record label) said that. But I think that makes it sound like it's boring, but it is actually a good description in a way.

Peanut: I think that description indicates a band thriving on the sound and the direction that they've found, you know? It's almost like we don't have to reinvent ourselves, we're just happy to let it grow the way it's growing.

Nick: Yeah, I mean if you've grown up from Kaiser Chiefs 'Employment' that's good. It isn't like growing up from a dadrock band or whatever. Where can you possibly go from there? Only in the direction of rugs on stage and no shoes! If you grow up from 'Employment', there's a lot of places to grow to. And from as well. And none of the new songs will have a bit where we go "Ohhhhhhh-h-hhhhhhhhhhhhhhh-OHHHHHHHHHHHHHHH!". None of them.

Though we used to think it was the Kaiser Chiefs sound, Whitey used to press this delay pedal on a particular setting and that was the Kaiser Chiefs sound and if we needed an exciting ending we'd go "Ohhhhhhhhhhhhh-hhhhhhhhh-OHHHHHHHHHHHHHHHHHH"!. We did it six times on our Japanese B-sides record!

"It's going to be a Kaiser Chiefs record, and it will be the best Kaiser Chiefs record released yet!"
RICKY

Ricky: I'm not worried, I don't feel any pressure. When we wrote the first one we didn't start off making sweeping statements. I hate that when people say, "It's going to be ballsy and more electronic!" There's no point saying that because the songs dictate that and you shouldn't push things in a way they don't want to go. It's going to be a Kaiser Chiefs record, and it will be the best Kaiser Chiefs record released yet!

Ricky: People talk about pressure, but there's none at all. It's fine. We're happy. The second album will be ready when it's ready and it will be better than the first one. We keep writing stuff, but we're not worried because we've achieved so much.

'When we were unsigned, that's when we felt it. Paying a fortune coming down to London and hoping A&R men would come and see you, that's pressure.